Black Widow Spiders

by Claire Archer

capstone®

ABDO
SPIDERS
Kids

Black Widow Spiders © 2016 by ABDO. All Rights Reserved. This version distributed and published by Capstone Classroom © 2016 with the permission of ABDO.

Photo Credits: iStock, Science Source, Shutterstock, Thinkstock

Production Contributors: Teddy Borth, Jennie Forsberg, Grace Hansen

Design Contributors: Candice Keimig, Laura Rask, Dorothy Toth

Library of Congress Cataloging-in-Publication data is available on the Library of Congress Website.

ISBN 978-1-4966-0979-3 (paperback)

Printed and bound in the USA.
009942F16

Table of Contents

Black Widow Spiders

Black widow spiders live around the world. You will likely find them in warm places.

4

5

Female black widows are black and shiny. They have red markings on their abdomens.

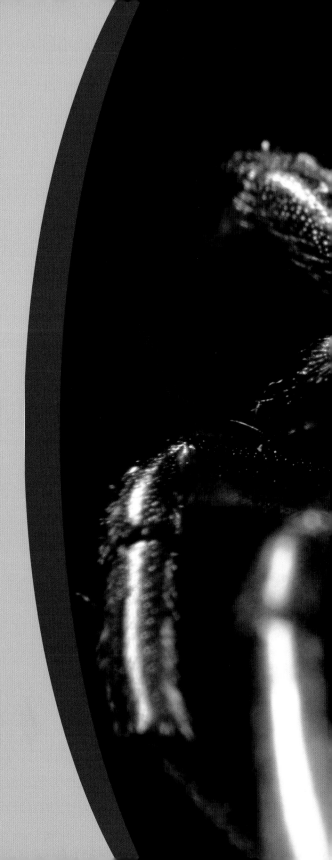

Male black widows are brown or gray. They have red dots on their bodies.

9

Males do not spin webs or eat. They only live for a month or two.

Hunting

Female black widows spin strong webs. Their webs trap unlucky prey.

12

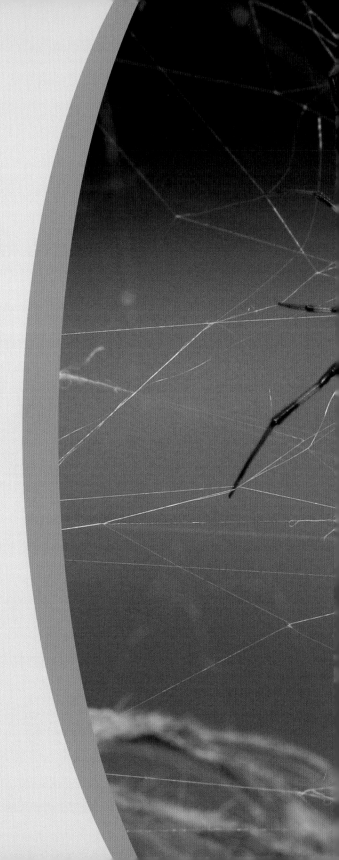

The female spins silk around her **prey**. Then she **injects** her prey with **venom**.

14

Food

Black widows mainly eat insects. They like flies, beetles, and more.

17

Baby Black Widow Spiders

A female spins silk around her eggs. This protects the eggs. The egg sac hangs from the web.

19

The female guards the eggs.

After they hatch, baby

spiders are on their own.

More Facts

- Black widows are **poisonous** spiders.

- Their poison is thought to be 15 times stronger than rattlesnake **venom**.

- Females hang upside down on their webs. This is to show their red markings. The red markings warn **predators**.

- Female black widows sometimes eat males. They got their name from this habit.

Glossary

abdomen – the back part of a spider's body.

egg sac – a protective silken pouch in which a spider puts her eggs.

inject – to force a liquid into prey's body through a bite.

poisonous – an animal that can produce poison to use against predators or prey.

predator – an animal that lives by eating other animals.

prey – an animal hunted or killed for food.

venom – a poison made by some animals.

Index